Foreword

Once again I have been privileged to b
fledgling writers have been on.

I have been blown away by the commitment and tenacity of the two
groups as they got to grips with the diverse writing prompts and
techniques thrown at them. What follows is a sample of eight weeks of
beautiful poetry and prose that has simply flowed from these
wonderful writers.

The sessions were held in two places and both groups have now
formed their own collectives – **The Watch Maker Writers** and
The Gallery Scribblers.

Watch out for them – I predict great things.

Susan Comer
Writer in Residence

This new phase of this still young project, has continued to broaden our
community offer and to reach out further. Serving as the new poetry and
writing platform for the borough and as a creative outlet for individuals
from all walks of life, it provides a positive and cathartic release,
communication and a reach out for collective understanding.

'From Pen to Paper' continues to be an intensely rewarding project for all
who comes in to contact with it.

Tina Ball
Chair of Friends of Kirkby Gallery & Prescot Museum

Participants

Sharon Briggs
Jane Evans
Lorraine France
Ruth Moane
Lisa Mogan
Ian Parnell
Jen Parr
Jane Peet
David Reynolds
Margaret Sanders
Ian Schofield
Jayne Schofield
Mark Shaw
Rita Simpson
Phil Waring
Rose Yates

Writer in residence: Susan Comer

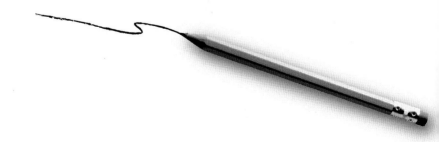

"The first draft is just you telling yourself the story."

Terry Pratchett

Sharon Briggs

A Woman's Lot

When we get to **the age** that women do,
oh the things that we have to look forward to,
grey hairs popping up on our head overnight,
look in the mirror get a **terrible fright**.

Boobs that nearly touch the bed as we sleep.
Wrinkles that are now ours to keep .
Needing the loo **5 times** through the night,
waking up early is all just hype.

Oh well looks like I don't have **a choice**,
but to grow old **disgracefully** in spite of myself.

01 05 11 13 16 18 21 30 40 50 60 65 70 80 90 100...

Jane Evans

NOW YOU SEE ME...

look, a wheelchair is what they see
no one bothers looking at me
they don't see a mum of four
so full of love my kids adore

they don't see I love to dance
heart full of want for fine romance
they don't see I love my wine
a bottle of red when I go out to dine

they don't see me laugh and cry
they just see me waiting to die
they don't see my family and friends
on which I can rely to the end

so next time you look and see the chair
take a look at me if you dare
you'll see me so full of fun
thank you for listening my poem is done

NOW YOU SEE ME... NOW YOU SEE ME... NOW YOU SEE ME... NOW YOU SEE ME... NOW YOU SEE ME...

Jane Evans

...BUT NOW YOU DON'T!

you sit in the corner all dark and moody
arm smooth shiny but oh so hard
threadbare treads touch the floor
drinking in all the life force you can take
weigh more than a heavy weight boxer
yet
with a feather light touch we spin on a sixpence
some call you the beast
I call you freedom

Lorraine France

SOCKS

Yer daft ditty Kitty, I can see yer socks,
Yer lovely shiny white clean tootsie paws stretching out
from underneath my pink flowering shrub,
You're so relaxed sleeping in the sun,
You know this garden's yours,
You own it - Boss.

You have the grey colouring of a cheetah cub,
the stripes, swagger and stalk of a tiger,
Wise piercing green eyes.
I am mesmerised as I watch you wait in opportunistic ambush.

The leaping frogs are just a game to practice your skills,
You clap your paws in satisfaction and let them go,
You really want a mouse or a small bird.

Now it's time to observe your prey,
Your demeanour changes to Killer Kat

You take a deep breath and
        stretch you whole body to look at its biggest,

            You pounce like a puma, a fast-short burst
            of speed and strength with expert precision,
        You clamp your claws around poor Robin,
        I have to look away and let nature takes its course.

                I've never stroked you in the years
                we have known each other,
                We have a mutual understanding.
                I know you're no Kute kitty.

            You return later in the day,
                your head hangs low,
                I can see a tuft of fur taken from your side,
        You've been in a Tom Kat Fight
        Licking your wounds but yer alright.

    I don't know who owns you,
    The amount of time you spend in my garden
    it may as well be me,
    You appeared out of nowhere to brighten up my life,
You know I love ya,
    daft ditty kitty who I've named **Socks**.

"You can always edit
a bad page.

You can't
edit a blank page."

Jodi Picoult

Ruth Moane

Limerick

There was a young man named Kyle,
Who's voice you could hear from a mile.
He smelt quite offensive,
Not the least bit attentive,
Yet he dazzled the girls with his smile.

Lorraine France

TWINKLE TOES

I looked out of the window and there you were,
Giving Socks the run around.
Chasing him up, chasing him down.
You looked so cute snuggled together beneath
the shade of the Buddleia tree.

The next day, sat on the roof of the shed
You spied Socks out of the corner of your eye,
turned your back and preened yourself.
Socks strutting up the lawn came to a standstill,
Eyes coyly diverted.
He sat underneath the rhubarb leaves,
mesmerised, adoringly gazing at you.

Majestically showing off your fluffy white chest,
You elegantly swayed in the most ladylike graceful way,
Youthful suppleness and agility well displayed.
Daintily tiptoeing on the grass, sidled up to Socks.
What a Kat Walk, "Very impressive"
You're one Kool Kitty, **"Twinkle Toes"**.

Mug of tea in hand,
I sat in my chair opposite,
You woke up startled, I smiled.
"You're very pretty, what a beautiful feminine feline
Lynx like face, perfect jawline".
Hazel eyes gazed at me.

Fetching smatterings of pretty pastel pink nose tip,
padded paws and ears that complement your sleek,
slinky light grey colouring.
Socks nonchalantly looked up at me,
yawned and went back to sleep.

Twinkle Toes and I are now best girlie friends,
I hear her tonal fluttering,
A soft scintillating purring sound as she circles around me,
brushing my legs with her tail.
She sweetly looks up at me.
I tell her all my secrets.

Socks looks a little jealous as he glances over at us girls,
He remains loyal and faithful,
That's the way we plan for it to stay.

"Start writing, no matter what.

The water does not flow
until the faucet is turned on."

Louis L'Amour

"Every secret of a writer's soul,
every experience of his life,
every quality of his mind,
is written large in his works."

Virginia Woolf

Lisa Mogan

The Meeting

A colony of **hens** gathered,

        Clucking to **share** their news.

A crescendo of **chatter**,

        A female flock **rooted** in rows.

A colourful display of **flowering** shrubs.

The **shrill cry** - a call to order,

    An abrupt bell-ring commanding **silence**

From the raucous, **squawking** prattle.

        Rising up obediently, like leaves

Caught **mid-flight** by the wind.

Mouths **poised**, open and ready

    To tweet the sweet familiar **birdsong**

That is **Jerusalem**.

Ruth Moane

The Favourite

She knows the one she wants.
No doubts,
no deliberation.

Back in her seat
she sits in quiet anticipation.
Such patience.

But now, her head turns
sharply as he approaches.
She sits taller in readiness.
Her delighted smile spreads
slowly to her eyes.
The moment is here.

She thanks him politely as he retreats
but keeps her focus.
Now utterly lost in the moment,
the little girl and her **favourite cake.**

"Don't tell me
the moon is shining;
show me the glint of light
on broken glass."

Anton Chekhov

Lisa Mogan

The Date

With eyes transfixed on the entrance door, Max's heart was racing. He shuffled on his chair for the nth time and checked his watch once again. He cupped his hands round the ridged ceramic coffee filled mug. The heat radiated through his fingers. He took a deep breath and lowered his eyes as he exhaled. This shouldn't have to be so daunting. It wasn't his first time. He knew what to expect. That was the problem. He hoped it would be different this time.

It had been a similar story on each previous occasion. The anticipation; the excitement, the anxiety; the disappointment. It was all down to one incident. The one that had changed his life forever.

It had all happened so fast. One minute he'd been on his way to get the morning paper. The next, he was lying in a hospital bed swathed in bandages. The firework had been casually tossed into his path. He didn't remember the explosion or the wailing sirens of the ambulance.

The first time he allowed himself to touch the left side of his face, he flinched. The smoothness of the tight skin contradicted by the fibrous ripples of scar tissue. It spanned from his temple in a wave down to his shoulder. It was a long time till he had the courage to face the mirror. Tears rolled down the red, angry welts as he contemplated the future. At twenty-five, he wasn't ready for defeat.

A tap on his right shoulder made him jump.

"Excuse me, are you Max?"

Startled, he half spun round to see a mass of curls framing stunning emerald green eyes. His heart raced even faster with panic. Will there be that familiar look when his whole face was revealed? Cautiously, he turned his head fully. Widening his eyes like a frightened rabbit, he looked for the answer.

"Er, y-yes," he stuttered, continuing to search for an indication that would give him an ounce of hope. A smile slowly erupted from each corner of their mouth. Suddenly he felt nervous. He'd not even got as far as buying coffee before, never mind making small talk.

Apprehensively, they took the opposite seat. "I'm really sorry, I've got a confession to make." Max froze. Holding his breath, he struggled determinedly to prevent the tears threatening to spill from his eyes.

"I've met you before. You probably don't remember." Max breathed out forcefully as he tried to recall.

"I was at the hospital when you were first admitted." Max was puzzled.

"I'm a nurse there, at the hospital. I looked after you for a short while." The explanation was a welcome relief.

"I've often wondered if I would ever see you again, and now here you are! It's a small world." The smile returned.

Max felt braver. "Let me get you a drink," he said, then hesitated, "I haven't even asked your name."

"It's Jack." The smile endured.

Max straightened his shoulders, "Hi Jack, it's really lovely to meet you. Finally."

Lisa Mogan

"And by the way,
everything in life is
writable about if you have the
outgoing guts to do it,
and the imagination
to improvise.
The worst enemy to creativity
is self-doubt."

Sylvia Plath

Ian Parnell

Nature

Nature's red in tooth and claw
The Heron knew as it stood in the pond
Life and survival, that's what it saw,
The surface looked still but the bird looked beyond

The gardener rose and walked round her estate
Passing the pool she saw nothing amiss
The fish swam on, unaware of their fate
But they'd all been touched with the Heron's hard kiss

The attack when it came was sudden and quick
The bird was impugn, rose above the law
Took every fish with a snap and a flick
The truth of our world is hard and it's raw,
Nature's red in tooth and claw.

Jenny Parr

Internal Bleeding

I rose, brushing off the dust,
Re-adjusting my limbs.
I edged across the road,
But they kept mowing me down as
I tiptoed across towards the pavement.

Too many bandages shielding the damage,
Covered up by polite smiles
I remove nightly.
But wounds won't heal.

"You're doing well," they say,
"Others have more pain,"
My clown face cracks,
I shiver with the ice, despite the sun.

I can't escape forever, I know,
soon the crows will swoop in,
to devour me as I sleep.
They have researched the final diagnosis.
Internal bleeding.

Jane Peet

BREAKFAST TIME

THE TOUCH OF THE
COOL, BULBOUS GLASS FEELS
FAMILIAR IN MY HAND AS I REMOVE THE
MORNING SUNSHINE LID REVEALING THE DARK
BOTTOMLESS MOLASSES-LIKE PASTE.

THEN I WELCOME THE SALTY, MALTY, MEDIEVAL
AROMA AND THE SCRAPING, GRATING ACROSS THE
CRUSTY TOAST THAT SCREAMS OUT 'BREAKFAST'.

FINALLY, THAT JOLT, THE SAVOURY TASTE OF HOME
FROM THAT FIRST BITE.

LOVE IT OR LOATH IT,
THIS IS **MARMITE**.

Jenny Parr

Advent

She had been awake since four am, writer's block! Words battered against the barrier around her brain. She needed a final sentence to finish her story, but nothing created a complete satisfactory ending. After more wasted hours, she got up, avoiding the clock, following a usual routine; shower, coffee and make up. She wrapped her dressing gown tighter around her shivering frame, looking outside to decide what to wear.

A panoramic scene of drifting snow met her gaze. As it danced on the window in twinkling flakes, she remembered the date, December the first; today she had a very important appointment. Dressing quickly, she pulled on her boots and rushed out.

Alfie sat on the floor doing a jigsaw. Every Christmas, he would get out his favourite one from the box under his bed. Every year he searched for the missing piece. It was a picture of Santa giving out presents to children sitting around a shining tree. He was holding out his hand containing a present, but Alfie could never make out what it was; just a space exposing the wood of the table underneath.

The other children in the home mostly ignored him; he could never find the words to ask them to be his friend, so he stayed alone and silent. He didn't believe in Santa now. Every year he asked for the same gift, but like the missing jigsaw piece, he never found it under the tree.

Mary arrived for the appointment flustered and red nosed with cold. A nervous excitement twisted her insides as she knocked on the imposing door. She was ushered into a lovely room full of Christmas decorations and warmth. After some small talk about the weather and shopping, Mrs Bell announced, *"I think we may have found a child for you. He is seven years old; we have found it difficult to find a home for him as most couples want a baby, but as you requested an older child, this should work well for you both. I have to tell you he has some problems with his hearing, but I'm sure with your patience and skill, communication will not be a problem."*

The door opened and in front of her stood a little boy with dark, troubled eyes, wide and scared.
"Alfie, this is Mary," she signed in his hand.
"Would you like to stay with her for Christmas, and if you're both happy, longer?"

His small hand stretched across the chasm of ocean and land. She took it in her own and signed, *"Merry Christmas, Alfie".* Their eyes met in recognition of missing words and jigsaw pieces.
"Maybe Santa listened," he thought, a smile pushing out of the corners of his pursed lips.

The barrier in her head broke away and words flowed through. She had found her final sentence.

And they lived happily ever after...

"It is perfectly okay
to write garbage

as long as you **edit** brilliantly."

C. J. Cherryh

Jane Peet

Introducing Honey

The nectar varnished coat is
melted with cloud like markings
placed on with precision by
St Francis himself.

The dark almond Bollywood
eyes that can break your heart,
or I've been told, lock on to an
enemy and send warning.

That freckled, daisy dotted
pigskin belly, polished with
tickles and once used to feed
too many young.

Flip flop ears responding to
a far off whisper with radar
precision. A turned up charcoal
nose which can smell a Malteser
from a mile away.

With her deep, broad, reassuring
tiger chest and her strong
sculptured limbs, she helps pull
me up the sand-hills like some
great Alaskan powerhouse.

Her whippedly-whip wand like
tail would put young Master
Potter to shame
and her overloaded grim,
chock-a-block with canine
happiness that any porpoise
would envy.

This is my dog

My rescue dog

But who rescued who?

David Reynolds

JUST ASK FOR HELP

WHEN YOU DON'T KNOW SOMETHING,
IF YOU DON'T KNOW WHERE SOMETHING IS,
IF YOU DON'T KNOW HOW MUCH SOMETHING IS IN THE SHOPS,
THE OVEN MAY BE BROKEN,
THE TELEVISION WON'T CHANGE CHANNELS ON THE REMOTE,
YOU WOULD RATHER GET LOST ON THE TUBE IN LONDON,
THAN APPROACH SOMEONE FOR ASSISTANCE,
IS IT OUR PRIDE,
DO WE EXPECT TOO MUCH OF OURSELVES?

JUST ASK FOR HELP

WHAT IS THIS, WHAT'S THE WORST THAT WILL HAPPEN IF
YOU DON'T KNOW SOMETHING,
THERE WILL BE NO EARTHQUAKE (*HOPEFULLY NOT ON THAT MINUTE*)
ALL YOUR TEETH WON'T FALL OUT ON THAT MINUTE,
A LION WONT RUN OUT ON THAT MINUTE
FROM THE SHOP WHICH YOU CAN'T FIND ANYWAY,
SURELY TO PREVENT ANXIETY OR TO GET LOST?

JUST ASK FOR HELP

IT TAKES AT TIMES A LOT OF STRENGTH TO SAY I CAN'T DO THIS,
AN EMAIL ON COMPUTER,
A TEXT ON A PHONE,
HOW TO BOIL AN EGG, HOW TO USE A NEW WASHING MACHINE,
HOW TO WRITE. HOW TO PASS AN EXAM AT SCHOOL,
THESE DAYS YOU NEED A BRILLIANT EDUCATION JUST SO YOU
KNOW HOW TO USE A WASHING MACHINE,
WHAT'S THE POINT IN A PRE-WASH,
WHAT'S WRONG WITH JUST A WASH?

JUST ASK FOR HELP

IT IS STRANGE WHEN I WAS SIXTEEN I KNEW EVERYTHING,
WELL I THOUGHT I KNEW EVERYTHING
IT SEEMS THE OLDER I GET THE LESS I KNOW.
IT IS NO GOOD PRETENDING I KNOW IN A MOMENT
I HAVE TO GO TO THE JOB CENTRE,
AND THE DOCTORS,
AND I KNOW HOW TO PROGRESS

I WILL *JUST ASK FOR HELP*

"Everybody walks past a thousand story ideas every day.

The good writers are the ones who see five or six of them. Most people don't see any."

Orson Scott

Ian Schofield

The Apple Tree

I first noticed you from my room with a view
You welcomed me to my new home
I know you see me when I look at you
A new friend, now I'm all alone

New leaflets of spring unfold a new year
A year we are starting anew
Were you aware, were you guiding me here?
Aware of what I'm going through

Catching the breeze you dance to and fro
Beckoning branches reach out
Season by season I'm watching you grow
But this dance I'll have to sit out

When autumn leaves fall and the year grows cold
And winter sleep calls unto you
Just rest for a while but I want you to know
I'll be waiting right here for you

Margaret Sanders

Machination Machination: *noun plural.*
conspiracy /design/scheme/trick

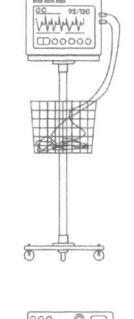

Existence and Machines.
Lying in my mechanical bed,
Dripping lines attaching me to
Traffic lights of go, stop and stay.
Listening to the pulsing beat of blood
Rushing around my veins.
Each machine sounding a delightful tone,
Pinging in their own special way.
Existing in a world of machines
Which I love yet fear.

Emotions and Machines.
I adore my washing machine
It knows me so well.
Clothes assessed in measured soap and water,
A very economical thirty degrees.

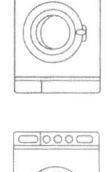

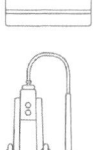

I tingle at the power of the carpet cleaner,
As it sucks away the dirt and grime of daily life.
And snatchers at the sly cobweb
In the corner of the room.

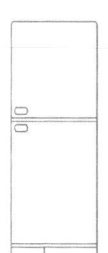

I regret the power of the near empty drum.
A half load wash of whites
Will not be done.
The call goes out for at least two more socks.

The pan and brush I fear to use.
The disapproval of the mighty Dyson, sensed as
I reach into that dark recess under the stairs.
I am obliged to plug in and run.

Contradictions and Machines
The pure white kitchen is innocent and virginal
Inviting in all things good and pure.
Its what we see on entering though the door,
An appearance of truth and reality.
Is that really how it seems?

The eye of the washing machine stares
An ancient one eyed Cyclops waiting to hypnotise its prey
The mouth of the oven door hangs open
Waiting to gobble up anything that passes by.
Is that really how it seems?

Daily life and its apparent contradictions
Seeing objects as they appear,
A given shape and form ,
Touch, pressure, sensations.
Is that really how it seems?

Jayne Schofield

Goodbye my friend

Julia stared out of the window.
The night was still - a time to reflect on
what today had brought.

Seeing John lying in his coffin. Still and
lifeless. She remembered his laugh,
his funny sense of humour,
his passion for animals.
All now just a memory.

She shouldn't have gone to see him.
She can't get his image out of her mind.
Why did she go?

She hadn't spoken to him for over ten years.
She needed to see him
one last time - she told herself.

She remembered coming home emotionally
drained after visiting her dad in the
care-home. Dad was failing fast; he was
diagnosed with dementia over four years ago.
It had taken its toll on Julia.

She had heard the news about John from a
Facebook message on her iPad.
'Jonny's died'
He was her brother's friend, but she had hit it
off with him instantly.
Was it Lenny, his loyal furry companion that
had made her take an instant like to him?

John had had it all. A thriving building
business; fast cars, a beautiful home - millions
in the bank. Julia hadn't known him then,
but had enjoyed hearing his stories.

Then John's mum Emily died. John had devoted
his life to her, and her death had hit him hard.
He started drinking and doing drugs - anything
to block the emptiness from his life.

His business collapsed, and then the bank took
back his home. He didn't care;
he was depressed and wanted to die.
He was an only child. His dad had passed on
seven years before and it was just him and his
mother Emily - and now she was gone......

and so was John.

Goodbye my friend

"Don't bend;
don't water it down;
don't try to make it logical;
don't edit your own soul
according to the fashion.

Rather, follow your most
intense obsessions mercilessly."

Franz Kafka

Phil Waring

Silent Billy

Fairground gold fish in a bowl
We'll take him home
And will call him Billy And teach him some new tricks. Swimming round and round Opens his mouth continually But doesn't make a sound. My dad thinks I'm being silly He forgets, I'm only six.

Ian Schofield

My Destiny
(Chok Chátá Kong Chan)

I wandered boldly through the crowds

The confusing world of Doe Ray Me

A barren wasteland filled my eyes

I wondered what was meant for me

Then I wandered lonely through the clouds

Crossed lands as far as the eyes could see

And chanced upon a Land of Smiles

Where special friends awaited me

Ian Schofield

Paradise Waits

I can taste the salt in the ocean spray
Feel the grains of the sand beneath my feet
See a glorious sunset that heralds the day
Smell the scent of the turquoise glistening sea

I can hear the call of the beckoning waves
In my dreams this is real, as real as can be
But will Tide and Time wait till I'm old and grey?
No, but Paradise Waits ..... and it's waiting for me

Mark Shaw

Valentina Must Choose

Valentina thought she wasn't doing too badly. Two breakfasts, two dinners and lots of extra snacks every day. But! And there always had to be a 'but' didn't there; Maude did try and smother her and control her life completely. And Mavis had Arthur. Oh Valentina simply couldn't abide Arthur. He was just so noisy and annoying and just plain stupid. Add to this the inconvenient truth that Maude and Mavis, neighbours for the best part of fifty years wouldn't even look at each other and right there you had the crux of the matter.

Poor Valentina was forced into a life of lies and secrecy. Sneaking from one house to the other. Living in fear of being exposed as a double agent. Subterfuge! And having to stuff her face with all that food! She would tell you none of this came natural to her. My goodness, she had her figure to think about.

But what could she do? She couldn't deprive either of the old dears of the love, affection and downright glamour she brought in to their lives. It would be unfair to choose one over the other. She had her cross to bear. She couldn't help it if everyone fell for her not inconsiderable charms. Everyone except Arthur that is.

Arthur had been watching Valentina for some time now. He thought she was being deceitful and sly. He knew what she was up to, playing both sides of the fence. He had to manage on one set of rations a day. Greedy Valentina was double dipping and playing fast and loose with the emotions of Mavis. Not to mention Maude next door. He knew the two women weren't talking but just couldn't understand why not. They'd be great company for each other if they could only get on. And he'd probably get more snacks.

When Valentina walked in he was ready for her. He pounced, knocking her down on to her back. Using his weight he pinned her down. She tried to escape but couldn't move. 'Get off you' she managed to gasp out. 'Shut up or I'll rip you to shreds' he said. 'I've been watching you little missy. I know your game. But I've got a plan that'll save your bacon and help me out too. Agree to it, or I'll have you for breakfast.'

Valentina was shocked beyond belief. How had this idiot found her out? She was totally trapped. She had to agree to his terms or she'd either be dead meat or caught out in her ruse. Reluctantly she accepted. She could always renege on the deal later – from a safe distance.

Arthur took her out in to the back yard. There he began to make the most frightful racket. Next thing she saw was Maude and Mavis at their back windows. Valentina was wondering what on earth Arthur was doing! 'Now!' he said 'jump on my back and I'll run around the yard with you.' She complied and thought now I've got you, I'm going to choke you by the throat! But as he ran and jumped around with her she began to laugh to herself at the absurdity of the situation. 'Look like your enjoying yourself' he said. But she didn't need to look like, she actually was enjoying herself.

The two neighbours came out from their back doors and looked on puzzled. But slowly Maude began to smile at the scene and when she turned to look at Mavis, Mavis too was standing in the doorway laughing to herself. The two old friends looked at each other across the fence and smiled at each other for the first time in a lifetime.
'Job done Valentina, you can get off me now.'
'No chance Arthur, I'm staying on.'

"I can shake off everything
as I write;
my sorrows disappear,
my courage is reborn."

Anne Frank

Rita Simpson

Acer Campestre

Dignified, majestic, soldier like.
A sturdy back bone and muscular limbs
Heading towards the sky.
Donning your autumn colours.
Lush green, red, pale yellow, russet brown, golden.
In the cool, still of the morning air
Silence pervades in the garden.
The golden rays strike the crown and shimmer
Contrasting against the clear blue sky.
Your finger tips painted with changing colours yellow among green.
A single leaf floats lazily downward
To join the blanketed earth below.
While the rising sun manoeuvres between the houses,

Speckling the lower limbs.
Midday sees you bathed in glowing embers.
Casting shadows across the lawn.
The wind's breathe strengthens,
Rustling, shaking, bending your spine.
Stripping limbs and scattering your cargo.
Far above skeletal arms reach out.
Below, the swirling castaways dance and frolic carelessly.
Catching in the spikes and crevices.
On the ground others wait to be crushed and crunched
By unthinking feet.
When evening arrives
A calm has settled around you.
Acer Campestre stands firm, tall and proud.
In its sandpaper covered
Weatherproof skin.

Rita Simpson

The Woman in Red

They were an **odd pair**. Him with his painted lips, matched the other dressed in **red** from the top of her head to her footwear. Each carried a **burden**. The young man with his large wooden guitar and the woman with her wriggling, scruffy looking mongrel tucked under her arm. I tried to work out the **relationship** between them. Months later I discovered they were **aunty** and **nephew**.

I first crossed their path in my favourite pub. Wednesday night was acoustic night which attracted local singers and songwriters. When his turn came, he **nervously** made his way to the mike. His **eyes** never met the audience as he sang a song of lost love followed by several more **morose** tunes. But the **red woman** clapped encouragingly while her dog drank from her pint glass. He grimaced as he returned to his seat, commenting to those nearby that his **ex-partner** had been a huge **mistake**.

"Never mind," said the woman. Then looking at me, "He's going to have one of my dog's puppies. I've got six others. They're **my life**." She hugged the dog and kissed its face. They left shortly after.

A few days later I was **surprised** to see the woman in red sat on the **pavement** in front of the Town Hall. Her dog sat next to her. She wore the exact same clothing. In front of her was a wooden bowl and a sign. '**HELP THE HOMELESS**.' Always unsure of whether to give, I **dropped** a couple of pound **coins** into her bowl. She nodded her thanks. For several weeks she became a regular feature on the high street. Then she **disappeared**.

The next time I saw her **face** was on the **front page** of the local newspaper. She'd been **murdered**. Her body was discovered in woodland on the edge of the town. Her **nephew** was in **custody**. An unnamed source was quoted as saying the murdered woman had been **forced** by her nephew to go out each day to **beg** so that they could buy food. The **motive** for her murder **wasn't known** but alongside her **body** were her beloved **dogs**. **All shot through the head**.

Rose Yates

My Cat

Poppy rules the roost!
She chooses when to like me
She chooses when to dislike me.
Poppy is unpredictable, independent.
She keeps me guessing.

The green eyes in her sweet little face
   Give no hint as to her feelings.
   Poppy purrs when tickled under her chin.
   This does not last as she stretches out
her claws to say 'STOP'.

If you have cheese, you are Poppy's friend.
She is right at your elbow until the very end.
She smells the aroma as it leaves the fridge.
And even tries to get onto the plate to reach her bit.

Poppy will pester when the computer's in use.
Moving the keyboard is no solution.
She sits mid screen for your full attention.
And watches the cursor for her next pounce!

Phil Waring

Iron Age

Ships sail in and ships sail out
Tide comes in and tide goes out
Sun comes up and sun goes down
And the moon will cross the sky.
We know how they feel
But "How do they feel?"
Barnacle encrusted – red, brown and rusted.
Hard rough coarse to touch.

Red and grey fur scurrying within and without
the decay of the autumn.
Leaves, gold, brown and yellow
Chill air on finger tips and evening sun, mellow.

Ships sail in and ships sail out
Tide comes in and tide goes out
Sun comes up and sun goes down
And the moon will cross the sky.
We know how they feel
But "How do they feel?"
Barnacle encrusted – red, brown and rusted.
Hard rough coarse to touch.

Woodland pine crane for scarce lit skies
And blue bells raise their heads
From the sands shrill, nervous laughter
Dunes become teenage beds

Ships sail in and ships sail out
Tide comes in and tide goes out
Sun comes up and sun goes down
And the moon will cross the sky.
We know how they feel
But "How do they feel?"
Barnacle encrusted – red, brown and rusted.
Hard rough coarse to touch.

Dad's off work and families play, tennis balls
Kites and frisbee, crowds on the beach are happy
And what floats by on low tide?
A loathsome, disposable nappy.

Ships sail in and ships sail out
Tide comes in and tide goes out
Sun comes up and sun goes down
And the moon will cross the sky.
We know how they feel
But "How do they feel?"
Barnacle encrusted – red, brown and rusted.
Hard rough coarse to touch.

Days, weeks, months and years pass by, each one
Just like the others
We have time to kill as the ages stand still
For me and my 99 brothers…
The ships sail in and the ships sail out.

Review and feedback

Meeting other people interested in writing. Listen to their ideas and sharing my own. It is very good for me, a good feel! Getting absorbed in writing. Meeting new people. - **Rita Simpson**

I feel more confident now and am encouraged to read and write more. I have been suffering from depression for three years and this has helped me express myself when I'm in a dark place and celebrate my good and great days. - **Jane Peet**

I am really enjoying listening to other peoples work and sharing my own. Helping each other with our feedback. - **Lorraine France**

It was inspired to have an experienced writer as the main lead of the group. Sue provided the lynch pin which enabled this group to develop as a writing forum but also allowed each individual scope to find their creative voice. - **Margaret Sanders**

It has been the best writing course I have been on and would highly recommend it to anyone. And I would love to do it all over again. - **Lisa Mogan**

Thanks for encouraging me to share my ideas/writing. I tend to lack self belief so it's nice getting positive feedback. I've surprised myself. - **Ruth Moane**

Just liked being linked up with other writers. - **Lesley Finney**

It was comfortable and relaxed. The tutor helped the group to grow into a writing group. - **Ian Parnell**

Lots of different people there, with different interests and tales to tell. Good to meet people from my community. Kirkby Gallery and Library is also a most welcoming building. - **Jane Peet**

*There was a feeling of mutual learning and co operation within the group and the course fostered this. - **Margaret Sanders***

I feel more confident sharing my work and in my writing.
- **Lorraine France**

*I have found new confidence. My self esteem was low before started course, now feel better. - **Jen Parr***

Flow of ideas was good, we learnt to exchange ideas.
- **Lesley Finney**

*I am always looking for courses, particularly locally and I really enjoyed it. - **Mark Shaw***

From introverts to extroverts, this course has a great deal to offer. I didn't know what was in my head until I put pent to paper and received positive results. - **Phil Waring**

*I now have confidence in reading my own work to others. Able to accept others ideas opportunities to become a writers group is great so we can continue to meet. - **Rose Yates***

Meeting lovely new people. Being encouraged to share work with the group. Positive feedback, non judgemental. Learning about prompts. - **Ruth Moane**

*Perfectly explained, steady paced. - **Jen Parr***

Writing prompts can spark off ideas, and are useful in loosening you up. Here are a few used during the From Pen to Paper writing course. Set your timer and finish the sentence – don't think about it first just write whatever comes into your head. Stick to the time and stop when the 2 or 3 minutes is up – even mid-sentence. Relax and enjoy the experience, you may surprise yourself!

3 minute prompt

Outside the Window:
What's the weather outside your window doing right now? If that's not inspiring, what's the weather like somewhere you wish you could be?

3 minute prompt

The Vessel:
Write about a ship or other vehicle that can take you somewhere different from where you are now.

3 minute prompt

Dancing:
Who's dancing and why are they tapping those toes?

....

....

....

....

....

....

....

....

....

....

....

....

....

....

....

....

3 minute prompt

Eye Contact:
Write about two people seeing each other for the first time.

2 minute prompt

The Rocket-ship:
Write about a rocket-ship on it's way to the moon or a distant galaxy far, far, away.

2 minute prompt

Dream-catcher:
Write something inspired by a recent dream you had.

2 minute prompt

Animals:
Choose an animal. Write about it!
Friendship: Write about being friends with someone.

2 minute prompt

Dragon:
Envision a dragon. Do you battle him? Or is the dragon friendly?
Use descriptive language.